It's Not Easy Being a Teenager

We wish to thank Susan Polis Schutz for permission to reprint the following poem that appears in this publication: "Always Create Your Own Dreams and Live Life to the Fullest." Copyright © 1988 by Stephen Schutz and Susan Polis Schutz. All rights reserved.

ISBN: 978-1-59842-835-3

▐▌ and Blue Mountain Press are registered in U.S. Patent and Trademark Office. Certain trademarks are used under license.

Acknowledgments appear on the last page.

Printed in China.
First Printing: 2014

♻ This book is printed on recycled paper.

This book is printed on paper that has been specially produced to be acid free (neutral pH) and contains no groundwood or unbleached pulp. It conforms with the requirements of the American National Standards Institute, Inc., so as to ensure that this book will last and be enjoyed by future generations.

Blue Mountain Arts, Inc.
P.O. Box 4549, Boulder, Colorado 80306

It's Not Easy Being a Teenager

Positive Thoughts

to Inspire Courage,

Confidence, and

Believing in Yourself

Edited by Patricia Wayant

Blue Mountain Press™

Boulder, Colorado

It's Not Easy Being a Teenager

Life doesn't always happen the way you want it to or the way you planned it or hoped for. Detours suddenly appear; storms blow in unexpectedly. The road you're traveling — that seemed so safe and secure — changes direction without warning, and life becomes something that's not at all what you thought it would be. You find there's nothing to do but stop for a while, figure out your options, and think about new decisions you have to make.

Life is forever changing. You can't always control what happens, but you can hang tough through it all and make the changes and decisions that are so necessary and will help you grow in spite of the disappointments, develop courage in spite of the adversities, be creative and come up with solutions, and always keep love in your heart.

No matter how hard things may seem... life will change again, and it's possible that this detour will lead you to a place that will bring you more happiness and let you reach more satisfying places in your heart and life than you've ever reached before.

■■ Donna Levine-Small

You Are Stronger Than You Know

When we go through life's struggles, we sometimes feel weak. It is as if we have forgotten the many things we have been through and how we have changed our lives before.

I am here to tell you that at this very moment, no matter what you are going through… you are stronger than you know.

Sometimes we don't know our power until the time comes to use it. It lies dormant within us and emerges just when we think we can't go on. And when it does, we find that we had much more power and strength than we ever thought possible.

So when you feel like giving up and throwing in the towel, know in your heart that your strength is on its way to the surface. One day you will look back at this moment and see just how strong you really were.

I promise, you are stronger than you feel and much stronger than you know.

:: Lamisha Serf

Always Create Your Own Dreams and Live Life to the Fullest

Get to know yourself
Find out who you are
Choose your goals carefully
Be honest with yourself
Always believe in yourself
Find many interests and pursue them
Find out what is important to you
Find out what you are good at
Don't be afraid to make mistakes
Work hard to achieve successes
When things are not going right
don't give up — just try harder

Give yourself freedom to
    try out new things
Laugh and have a good time
Open yourself up to love
Take part in the beauty of nature
Be appreciative of all that you have
Help those less fortunate than you
Work toward peace in the world
Live life to the fullest
Create your own dreams and
follow them until they are a reality

                 ∷ Susan Polis Schutz

Show the World Who You Are

*E*ach day that you are blessed with is precious. Don't waste a moment of today thinking about the past, trying too hard to change the present, or worrying too much about the future.

Embrace today. Look at the world through a lens of goodness, grace, and beauty. Accept yourself. You are enough, just as you are at this very moment.

Keep striving. Keep growing. Keep experiencing all that life has to offer. Keep hope alive in your heart. Keep a smile on your face, and stay on the path of all that is good and true in this world.

Be who you are and don't allow others to define you. Stop trying to please everyone. Do your best to finally please yourself.

You are special. You are blessed. You matter. Make the most of every precious moment you have been given. Gather those moments together and weave your life into a beautiful tapestry that is rich with love.

Live your life. It is sacred. Dream your dreams, make your mark... and show the world you are here.

:: Carole R. Dowhan

Don't Give Up
on Yourself

Life has a way of throwing us off course,
surprising us into making changes
we weren't planning on making.
Things may get difficult,
and you may struggle to do what's right.
But each new day brings new hope
and offers us a new chance to get it right.
Don't focus on what was.
Look forward to what can be,
and then do all you can to make it a reality.
Life is what you make of it,
and the challenges that come your way
are just opportunities to right what is wrong.
Don't get discouraged, and don't give up.
You have it all inside yourself,
and you can overcome anything
if you put your mind to it.

▪▪ Paula Michele Adams

On Being
a Champion

A champion is a winner,
A hero…
Someone who never gives up
Even when the going gets rough.
A champion is a member of
A winning team…
Someone who overcomes challenges
Even when it requires creative solutions.
A champion is an optimist,
A hopeful spirit…
Someone who plays the game,
Even when the game is called life…
Especially when the game is called life.
There can be a champion in each of us,
If we live as a winner,
If we live as a member of the team,
If we live with a hopeful spirit,
For life.

■■ Mattie J.T. Stepanek

Kids Who Are Different

Here's to the kids who are different,
the kids who don't always get As,
the kids who have ears twice the size
   of their peers'
or noses that go on for days.

Here's to the kids who are different,
the kids that are just out of step,
the kids they all tease,
who have cuts on their knees
and whose sneakers are constantly wet.

Here's to the kids who are different,
the kids with a mischievous streak,
for when they are grown,
as history has shown,
it's their difference that makes
them unique.

■■ Digby Wolfe

What Is a Teenager?

A teenager is a person who is part child and part adult.

A teenager is someone who loves to have fun and thrives on excitement, yet sometimes feels overwhelmed by new responsibilities and expectations.

A teenager is someone who is still learning from the past and is unsure about the future.

A teenager is someone who craves friends and an active social life, yet finds that you can't please everyone.

A teenager is someone who needs someone in his or her life who is a good example, who can be trusted with secrets, who is an avid listener.

A teenager is someone who needs to know that life always gets better and that things worth having are worth working and waiting for.

A teenager is someone who needs to
    understand that trying, combined with
    persistence and determination, are the
    biggest parts of succeeding and that
    mistakes are okay as long as you learn
    from them.

In between the joy of being a protected,
    cherished child
and the contentment of being a free,
    independent adult
is the fun, the frustration,
the confusion, the boredom,
the excitement, the despondence,
and the elation of a teenager.

                                        ❚❚ Barbara Cage

When You Feel Lonely...

Look up at the stars
and see the infinite number of them.
Remember how many people's lives
you have touched.
Look at your hands and remember
how many people they have helped.
Think of all the friends
you have laughed and cried with.
Remember all the friends who turned to you
when they were lonely too.

When you are lonely,
look at your arms and remember
all those whom they have held —
the ones who love you,
the ones who trust you,
and the ones who see you
for who you really are.

When you feel lonely,
remember that you are never alone.

:: Amanda Rowe

I Belong

I belong to the human race, but more importantly,
I belong to a spiritual race where there are
no color, language, or social barriers.

From this vantage point
I see myself as a link in the chain of life —
a chain that will be as weak or as strong as I am...

To make sure that the chain is strong,
I make myself strong.

I know that I am strong when I am happy,
so I do what makes me happy.

I ask myself what happiness means to me,
and I realize that it is love, peace, and harmony.

I think of how I can achieve them,
and the answer is clear:
I want love, so I give love.
I want peace, so I give peace.
I want harmony, so I wish for all
what I wish for myself; I wish only well.

∷ Carmen Colombo

Never Stop Growing

When you think you know it all, then you deny yourself the opportunity to learn anything new. When you decide that you've seen it all, you cut yourself off from new and enlightening experiences.

Every day is an opportunity to grow. Always take advantage of that opportunity, for it is a big part of what makes you alive.

No matter how much you've already accomplished, you can still receive great benefit from new challenges. No matter what your level of learning and experience, you can always raise that level even higher.

When you think you have all the answers, get busy and find some more questions. View each new discovery as a starting point, and not as a final destination.

The joy of life is in the journey. The fulfillment of life is in the growing.

Keep that growing going, and never let it stop.

∷ Ralph S. Marston, Jr.

There are no limitations in what you can do except the limitations in your own mind as to what you cannot do.

∷ Darwin P. Kingsley

It's Okay to Be Sad Sometimes

Don't be frightened if a sadness confronts you larger than any you have ever known, casting its shadow over all you do. You must think that something is happening within you, and remember that life has not forgotten you; it holds you in its hand and will not let you fall. Why would you want to exclude from your life any uneasiness, any pain, any depression, since you don't know what work they are accomplishing within you?

■■ Rainer Maria Rilke

The Guest House

This being human is a guest house.
Every morning a new arrival.

A joy, a depression, a meanness,
some momentary awareness comes
as an unexpected visitor.

Welcome and entertain them all!
Even if they're a crowd of sorrows,
who violently sweep your house
empty of its furniture,
still, treat each guest honorably.
He may be clearing you out
for some new delight.

The dark thought, the shame, the malice,
meet them at the door laughing,
and invite them in.

Be grateful for whoever comes,
because each has been sent
as a guide from beyond.

■■ Rumi

When Your Heart Gets Broken (and It Will)...

There's no reason to wear a goofy, smiley face to convince the world that you are just fine. You need to give this a chance to sink in and to become real for you. That may take a day or a weekend or even a week. Right now, the only person that matters is you. If you keep what you're feeling bottled up inside, you will not be able to start your healing process. So let it out, and don't be afraid to feel.

Pull your knees into your chest and wrap your arms around them tightly to keep you from falling apart. Then slowly let them go. You will find that with your feet spread out in front of you, with your limbs free and flowing, you are still whole. This is part of the acceptance, the realization that this relationship has come to an end — and miraculously, you are still alive.

:: Diane Mastromarino Jensen

$\int$ake the time to be alone,
so you can know just how terrific
your own company can be.
Remember that being alone
doesn't always mean being lonely;
it can be a beautiful experience
of finding your creativity,
your heartfelt feelings,
and the calm and quiet peace
deep inside you.

■■ Jacqueline Schiff

Tell Yourself "I Can"

Thinking you can do something
is the difference between
success and failure.
Wanting to do something
and believing you can do it
are two entirely different things.
It is best for them to go hand in hand
when we make a plan for our lives.
Sometimes we want something badly,
yet we doubt that we can ever achieve it.

It all starts with a thought — "I can."

You can do many things
that you never thought possible,
if only you change your mind.
Change the little voice in your head
that gives you all the reasons it isn't possible.
Replace them with positive, affirming thoughts
that give you encouragement along the way.
What you want to do is possible,
and you can do it.
Just believe.

If you can't completely believe it
right this very moment,
start small and replace
"I can't" with "I can."
The more you say it,
the more you will believe it.
And one day you will find
that you really mean it.

:: Lamisha Serf

You Can Handle Whatever Challenge You Have to Face

*W*hen you're having trouble with worry and you're about to give up, don't let it get the best of you — outsmart it. Say… "Okay, Worry, I'll give you ten minutes in the morning and ten minutes in the afternoon, but that's all the time you get from me and that's that. You will not steal my peace and cheat me out of my rest, and if you try to show up some other time, you'll just have to leave."

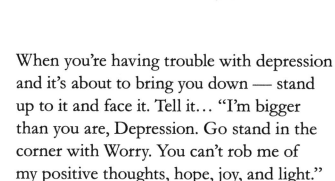

When you're having trouble with depression and it's about to bring you down — stand up to it and face it. Tell it… "I'm bigger than you are, Depression. Go stand in the corner with Worry. You can't rob me of my positive thoughts, hope, joy, and light." Show it who's the boss with your words and actions. Don't give in to it. Get busy doing something constructive, perhaps something you don't want to do but should, and you will feel empowered.

Talk to yourself. Be your own best friend. You have the power to overcome whatever challenge you face.

:: Donna Fargo

Don't Underestimate the Value of a Friend

A friend is someone who listens without judging you right or wrong, good or bad, and gently helps you define your thoughts to regain perspective.

When you're feeling bad about yourself, a friend is there to remind you of all those positive qualities you may have forgotten.

When you share with a friend, decision-making becomes easier and problems seem less critical.

A friend gives you the priceless gift of time: time to share, to try out new ideas and rethink old ones. No matter how often you're together, you discover dimensions of yourself through the bonds and the mirror of friendship.

A friend loves you for who you are, not what you do. Feeling so accepted, you are able to set higher goals, try harder, and achieve more.

Through close friendship, you learn the fine art of giving. You expand, become more selfless, feel more deeply, and help more effectively. Seeing the happiness you bring to another person gives you a greater sense of well-being and increases your capacity to love.

Wherever you go in life, whatever stage or place you reach, a friend who has entered your soul is always with you, gently guiding, faithfully following, and ever walking beside you.

▪▪ Sandra Sturtz Hauss

Always Be Ready for the Next Adventure

*N*ever stop reading, researching, and asking questions; always remain curious and keep learning. This is the learning curve you will be on forever. To keep learning, do this until the day you die: go everywhere (and I mean everywhere!) and experience as much as you can. Grab any opportunity to travel, look for opportunities to meet someone interesting, attend a lecture, go to a conference, or visit a distant friend or relative.

Do anything to get out of your comfort zone; try everything. Agree to do things you don't know how to do, and you will learn as you go. Take risks. One of my mottos is "identify the fear and then go there." Yes — with doubts, a pounding heart, a dry mouth, and butterflies in your stomach, but go and do the best you can.

If you fall flat on your face, get up, dust yourself off, and keep going. It just becomes part of the experience of that step you just left behind. If you never fail, it means you are not taking risks.

Be the one who gives credit when due, who gives advice and encourages, who can be relied upon to be helpful when needed. No matter how low you are on the ladder of life, there is someone below you just as there is someone above — and both are equally important. Be involved in your community — making friends, volunteering, and providing service where needed.

While all this may seem overwhelming, it is not something you do tomorrow in one fell swoop. It is a philosophy of life, a way of being. Always be ready for the next adventure.

Natasha Josefowitz

Choose Happiness

Happiness is a privilege in life. It's easy to be negative and stay negative, to criticize and complain, to see the glass as half empty rather than half full. To choose happiness is to be positive, to see the best in people, and to make the best of difficult situations.

To be happy is to share with others and give back in whatever way we can. To be happy is to live without regrets, to learn from our mistakes and move on. To be happy is to laugh more and worry less.

To be happy is to spend time with loved ones while being in complete awareness of how valuable that time truly is. To be happy is to exercise gratitude every day and feel good about ourselves, knowing that we're important in the world and that we exist for a reason. To be happy is to not compare ourselves to others, knowing that it doesn't matter what others think of us as long as we think good things about ourselves.

Choose happiness. It's an easy choice.

■■ Debbie Burton-Peddle

Believe

The dreams in your heart
are waiting to come true.
Give them wings —
and be all that you
could hope to be.
You can accomplish
more than you've ever imagined —
    as long as you believe.

There's no end
to the amazing things you can achieve —
if you set your mind to it.

Make a plan, and then —
one step at a time —
take the actions
that will bring your dreams to life.

Create the life
that you have always wished for —
because that is the life
that you deserve.

Follow your dreams!

■ Jason Blume

You're on the Journey of a Lifetime...

A journey no one else will travel and no one else can judge — a path of happiness and hurt, where the challenges are great and the rewards even greater.

You're on a journey where each experience will teach you something valuable and you can't get lost, for you already know the way by heart.

You're on a journey that is universal yet uniquely personal, and profound yet astonishingly simple — where sometimes you will stumble and other times you will soar. You'll learn that even at your darkest point, you can find a light — if you look for it. At the most difficult crossroad, you'll have an answer — if you listen for it. Friends and family will accompany you part of the way, and you'll walk the rest by yourself... but you will never be alone.

Travel at your own pace. There'll be time enough to learn all you need to know and go as far as you're meant to go. Travel light. Letting go of extra baggage will keep your arms open and your heart free to fully embrace the gifts of the moment.

You may not always know exactly where you're headed, but if you follow the desires of your heart, the integrity of your conscience, and the wisdom of your soul… then each step you take will lead you to discover more of who you really are, and it will be a step in the right direction on the journey of a lifetime.

▪▪ Paula Finn

Acknowledgments

We gratefully acknowledge the permission granted by the following authors and authors' representatives to reprint poems or excerpts from their publications:

Carole R. Dowhan for "Show the World Who You Are." Copyright © 2014 by Carole R. Dowhan. All rights reserved.

Hachelte Book Group for "On Being a Champion" from JOURNEY THROUGH HEARTSONGS by Mattie J.T. Stepanek. Copyright © 2001 by Mattie J.T. Stepanek. All rights reserved. Reprinted by permission of Hachelte Book Group.

Patricia Mannion-Wolfe for "Here's to Kids Who Are Different" from "Growing Pains" by Digby Wolfe from A LOTUS GROWS IN THE MUD by Goldie Hawn. Copyright © 2005 by Digby Wolfe. All rights reserved.

Barbara Cage for "What Is a Teenager?" Copyright © 2014 by Barbara Cage. All rights reserved.

Amanda Rowe for "When You Feel Lonely...." Copyright © 2014 by Amanda Rowe. All rights reserved.

Carmen Colombo for "I belong" (wowzone.com: 1996). Copyright © 1996 by Carmen Colombo. All rights reserved.

Ralph S. Marston, Jr., for "Never Stop Growing." Originally published in "The Daily Motivator" at www.dailymotivator.com. Copyright © 2005 by Ralph S. Marston, Jr. Reprinted by permission. All rights reserved.

Coleman Barks for "The Guest House" by Rumi from THE ESSENTIAL RUMI: NEW EXPANDED EDITION, translated by Coleman Barks. Copyright © 2004 by Coleman Barks. All rights reserved.

Lamisha Serf for "Tell Yourself 'I Can.'" Copyright © 2014 by Lamisha Serf. All rights reserved.

PrimaDonna Entertainment Corp. for "You Can Handle Whatever Challenge You Have to Face" by Donna Fargo. Copyright © 2014 by PrimaDonna Entertainment Corp. All rights reserved.

Natasha Josefowitz for "Always Be Ready for the Next Adventure" from "Life After Graduation" (*LaJolla Village News*: June 7, 2012). Copyright © 2012 by Natasha Josefowitz. All rights reserved.

Debbie Burton-Peddle for "Choose Happiness." Copyright © 2014 by Debbie Burton-Peddle. All rights reserved.

Jason Blume for "Believe." Copyright © 2014 by Jason Blume. All rights reserved.

A careful effort has been made to trace the ownership of selections used in this anthology in order to obtain permission to reprint copyrighted material and give proper credit to the copyright owners. If any error or omission has occurred, it is completely inadvertent, and we would like to make corrections in future editions provided that written notification is made to the publisher:

BLUE MOUNTAIN ARTS, INC., P.O. Box 4549, Boulder, Colorado 80306.